Ashmolean hand

CW00765843

Scythian and Thracian antiquities

in Oxford

Michael Vickers

Ashmolean Museum Oxford
2002

ISBN 1 85444 180 9 (paperback)
ISBN 1 85444 181 7 (papercased)

Ashmolean handbooks series
Series editor: Timothy Wilson
Publishing consultant: Ian Charlton

Titles in this series include:
The Ashmolean Museum
Drawings by Michelangelo and Raphael
Ruskin's drawings
Samuel Palmer
J.M.W. Turner
Camille Pissarro and his family
French drawings and watercolours
Oxford and the Pre-Raphaelites
Twentieth century paintings
Miniatures
English Delftware
Worcester porcelain
Eighteenth-century French porcelain
Maiolica
Islamic ceramics
Indian paintings from Oxford collections
Ancient Greek pottery
Glass of four millennia
Finger rings from ancient to modern
Frames and framings

British Library Cataloguing in Publication Data
A catalogue record for this book is available from the British
Library

Cover illustration: Scythian warrior, designed by E.Chernenko and
drawn by V.Bondareva; computer graphics by A.Kokorina

Designed and typeset in Versailles by Roy Cole, Wells
Printed and bound in Singapore by Craft Print International Ltd

Foreword

This booklet presents two of the most important groups of material in the Department of Antiquities at the Ashmolean Museum, namely the remarkable assemblage of Scythian grave goods from Nymphaeum presented to Oxford University by Sir William Siemens in 1880, and the contents of a Thracian princely burial from Dalboki, near Stara Zagora, Bulgaria: both from countries on the Black Sea. The Scythian material was first published *in toto* in my *Scythian Treasures in Oxford* (cited below as Treasures; it is now out of print, but can be read at: http://www.ashmol.ox.ac.uk/ash/oopp/Scythian Treasures/). While the Thracian finds have been discussed by Russian (Prochorov 1880) and Bulgarian colleagues (Filov 1930–31; Dimitrov 1950), this is the first time they have been presented at length in English.

Other museums outside Ukraine or Russia may have Scythian jewellery, but the Ashmolean is alone in having more or less complete grave inventories comprising not only jewellery but also silver plate, bronzework and pottery. Some of the material is of native manufacture but much of it seems to have been made by Greek craftsmen, and we thus gain an unexpected insight into a society in transition from what had been a nomadic, steppe-dwelling existence to an urban life on the edge of the Mediterranean world. Similarly, museums in Bulgaria have rich holdings of Thracian material (the gold and silver hoards of Panagyurishte and Rogozen being perhaps the best known), but the Ashmolean's holdings are the most significant in what used to be called the West. The degree to which the world has changed since 1989 may be judged by the

3

fact that the Museum now has its own excavation, run jointly with Georgian colleagues, at Pichvnari on the eastern shore of the Black Sea.

The photographs are the work of David Gowers and Nick Pollard of the Ashmolean's photographic studio. Julie Clements, Manana Odisheli, Darejan Kacharava, Sophie Stos, Evgeni Chernenko, Valeria Bylkova, Lars Sewilius Berg, Carly Jones and Cornelia Ewigleben provided invaluable help. David Braund and Tim Taylor kindly read through the text at proof stage, but any shortcomings are the responsibility of the author.

Michael Vickers, Professor of Archaeology

Scythian antiquities

In June 1868, Messrs Siemens Bros. of London were granted the contract to lay a new telegraph line from the Prussian frontier to Tehran. It was to run for some 4000 km through Russian and Persian territory, and part of its route lay across the straits of Kerch from the Crimea to the Kuban peninsula. In December 1868 some tumuli in the necropolis of the city of Nymphaeum were explored by Franz Biller, who was Siemens' agent in the area. By the standards of the time, Biller's excavations were exemplary, and his record-keeping first rate. His approach will have been an advance over that of his immediate predecessors at Nymphaeum; tomb-robbing had

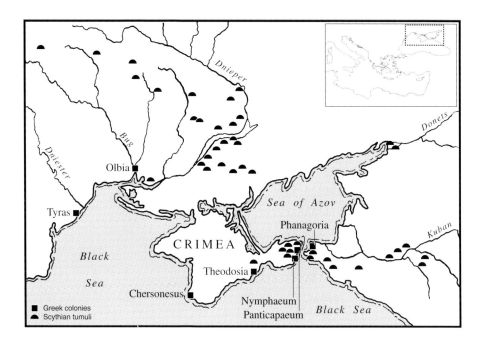

been going on since 1867, and some of the finds had been confiscated and taken to the Hermitage (Rostovtzeff 1931, 344). The main object of Biller's excavations were the rich contents of the tombs over which the tumuli had been constructed; these included armour, rings, bracelets, necklaces and pottery. Biller's discoveries were offered for sale to A.Lyutsenko, the Director of the Museum of Antiquities at Kerch, but the price (at 3,000 roubles) was considered to be too high. Lyutsenko did, however, submit a report to the Imperial Archaeological Commission in St Petersburg (*Treasures* 1979, 53–4), and also published a short note in a Muscovite archaeological journal in 1870 (Lyutsenko 1870; *Treasures*, 51–2).

The objects were acquired by Biller's employer, Sir William Siemens the engineer, who was in the Crimea in June and July of 1869 supervising the laying of the Kerch part of the Indo-European Telegraph in person (Pole 1888, 177). In 1870 Siemens was granted an honorary doctorate by the University of Oxford in recognition of his engineering achievements, and when some years later he was looking for a place where the Nymphaeum assemblages would be accessible to the public, he deposited them on loan at the University Museum at Oxford. In an accompanying letter, he stated that: 'What adds to their value is the circumstance that the Russian Government have reserved the right of searching these graves to themselves and have only made an exception in my favour under exceptional circumstances'. During their first few months in Oxford, the Nymphaeum finds played a part in the propaganda war surrounding the creation of a 'Home of Archaeology in Oxford' at the Ashmolean Museum (Evans 1884).[1]

In 1884, Siemens presented all the Nymphaeum finds to the University of Oxford, and by 1885 everything (with the exception of the human skeletal material) was transferred to the Ashmolean. The cranium and mandible were recovered from the British Museum, Natural History in 1978. Thanks to

[1] '. . . this year other Greek earrings and a noble gold necklace appear close to some models of Intestines in the Natural History Museum. No donor's name is appended to these last, but a card sets forth the simple and highly intelligible fact that they were found at "Gurgan". It is possible that some of the most learned Heads of Houses might be able to state forthwith where "Gurgan" is, but the mystery must be great to many in *statu pupillari*, and, in pity for the unlearned, one is justified in craving a more descriptive label' (Chester 1881, 8)

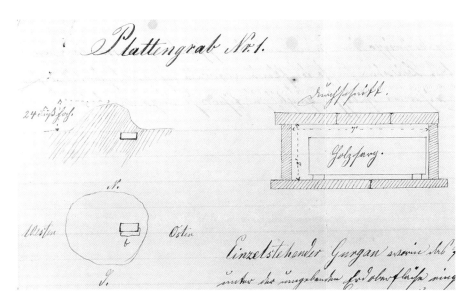

Biller's careful records, which described his activities at Nymphaeum in some detail, and Lyutsenko's report and published note (Lyutsenko 1870) it has been possible to reconstruct the inventories of six graves with a fair degree of certainty (see *Treasures*), although Biller speaks of only five. An earlier account by E. A. Gardner was made without the benefit of documents in Russia (Gardner 1884), or without the knowledge that the cranium and mandible from Grave I (which were taken to be from the same skull) are of a man and a woman respectively. Lyutsenko's report was once accompanied by drawings by 'the painter Gross', but these are now lost. Nevertheless, taking all the primary sources as well as the objects into account we can construct a picture of the tumuli, the graves and their contents as follows:

Grave 1: Warrior and woman
The grave was constructed with slabs of roughly worked local limestone and was situated in the Southeast quadrant of a tumulus (kurgan) twenty-four feet (7.25 m) high, about two feet (60 cm) below surrounding ground level (Fig. 1). The skeletons of a

dog and a horse lay on top of the grave slabs. The grave was aligned from east to west, with the heads at the east end. There was a coffin 'of walnut' held together with wooden dowels, with a moulding around the upper edge. A double burial, a male and a female, apparently laid one on top of the other. The cranium of one (Plate 1, below left) and the mandible of the other (Plate 1, below right) survive.

(a) The man seems to have been a warrior, and to him can be attributed a large number of arrow-heads, twenty-two bronze and one bone (Plate 2), whose shafts of reeds were excavated but have not survived. It is reasonable to give to him the helmet (Plate 1, above) which is not mentioned in any of the written accounts. For a reconstruction of what the warrior may have looked like, see the front cover.

(b) The woman's goods were rather richer, and included a pair of boat-shaped earrings (Plate 3), a small plain electrum ring (Plate 20, middle), a necklace of eight small boxes of sheet gold with pendants in the form of beechnuts (lost), a small bronze mirror (Plate 4, below), two marble alabastra (lost), and an Attic red-figure lekythos (Plate 4, above). There were at least eighty-four small appliqués in the form of hares (Plate 5) originally sewn on to a garment, and there was a great deal of organic material preserved: animal skins, woollen thread, samples of which are now in Oxford (Plate 6), pieces of sponge and nuts.

Grave 2: Woman

Found in a small tumulus eighteen feet (6.45 m) high, one of a row of tumuli. The grave, presumably stone-built like the last, was situated in the eastern part of the tumulus and was at surrounding ground level. There was a wooden coffin with 'two decorative motifs' visible on one side. The head of the deceased lay to the east, and at the neck there was a necklace of gold rams' heads (Plate 7, above), there were gold circular earrings at the shoulder (Plate 7, below) and on the right hand a gold ring with an intaglio of a sphinx (Plate 7, middle). The pots men-

8

tioned by Biller are probably the *askoi*, cups and
lekanis in Plates 8 and 10, below; one of them has
the name Achaxe beneath in Greek (Plate 9, below).

Grave 3: Woman

Found in a small tumulus lying east to west. There
was a wooden coffin, and two silver bracelets (Plate
11, below) and a small necklace (Plate 11, above).

Grave 4: Woman

Found in the Southwest quadrant of a large tumulus, some two to three feet (60–90 cm) below the surrounding ground level. The grave was stone-built,
and seven feet (2.10 m) long. It contained a wooden,
undecorated coffin. A necklace (Plate 12, above) was
found on the breast and there were two hair ornaments at the shoulders (Plate 12, above). There were
also an engraved finger ring (Plate 18, below) and at
least forty-nine appliqués in the form of small gold
lions (Plate 13) found scattered over the body and
formerly, no doubt, sewn on to a garment. A small
silver cup (Plate 15, above) lay near the left hand and
close by, a washing sponge (lost). On the right, a
patera (Plate 14, below left) and a mirror (Plate 14,
below right). Outside the foot-end of the coffin were
found wooden cups, two spindles and the remains
of a chair (all lost).

Grave 5: Woman

Found in a fairly large tumulus by the seashore.
There was a wooden coffin, in which were a finger
ring (Plate 18, below left or Plate 18 below right,
Fig. 12 or 13) and a chalcedony scaraboid (Plate 15,
below) perhaps worn around the neck.

Grave 6: Warrior

Found in a tumulus, the burial was in a wooden coffin with the head to the east. At the neck there was
an electrum torc (Plate 18, above); on the chest,
scale armour (Plate 17, above) decorated with a solid
bronze plaque in the form of an elk's head (Plate 16).
On the legs bronze greaves without decoration

(Plate 17, below). By the legs there was probably a corroded iron sword. There was also a bronze ladle (probably the one in Plate 19, left) and three black-glaze pottery vessels (*not* those in Plates 9; 10 above; 10 below, and Figs 6–8, for Lyutsenko's account specifies two *paterae* and a cup with a high foot).

So much for the known grave-groups. There are some objects amongst the Scythian material in Oxford which are not accounted for or whose attribution to a grave-group is not certain on the basis of the descriptions we have. The helmet (Plate 1, above) has been mentioned already, but it almost certainly belongs to Grave I. The glass alabastron (Plate 19, right) is not specifically mentioned in any of the accounts; it could not be one of the 'tear-flasks' mentioned in connection with Grave I, for they were reported to have been of marble and were decayed. The fine bracelets with rams' heads terminals (Plate 11, below) surprisingly are not connected with any of the graves in the accounts we have, although Gross made a drawing of one of them. Some rings, too, lack a precise provenance. Grave IV is said to have included an 'engraved' finger ring, but it is not clear whether it was the head of a bearded man seen from the side (Plate 18, below left, Fig. 10) or the head of a youth shown frontally (Plate 18, below right, Fig. 11). There is also an extra plain gold ring. There are two in all (Plate 20, middle left and Figs. 12 and 13), but it is impossible to say which is which. Nor do we know to which graves the small gold mask of a woman (Plate 20, below right) or the two circular electrum bosses (Plate 20, below left) belong.

These graves are typical of those found in the necropolis at Nymphaeum (see Silantyeva 1959, *passim*; Gajdukevič 1971, 289–92; Grach 1999; Scholl and Zin'ko 1999). Some may have been more elaborate: there was one, for instance, found in 1876 (Tumulus 24) which had the skeletons of eight horses arranged around the burial chamber, two on each side. Near the skeletons were many pieces of iron and bronze harness and trappings (Silantyeva 1959,

68–9, fig. 37), including the stylised heads of birds and a boar, made rather after the fashion of our elk plaque in Grave VI (Plate 16). The wooden coffin had inlaid decoration and in it was the skeleton of a warrior. Around his skull were fifteen gold appliqués (ibid., fig. 24.4–9) rather more diverse in character than ours: a ram's head, the head of an ape, a gorgoneion, a flying eagle, a seated sphinx, etc. Around his neck was a gold torc (ibid., fig. 24.1) similar to ours (Plate 18, above), and on his left hand a gold ring with a Greco-Persian scaraboid (ibid, fig. 24.2, cf. Plate 15, below). Outside the sarcophagus there was iron and bronze armour including iron swords, daggers and spearheads. There were in addition a fragmentary silver phiale (ibid., 58, fig. 26; cf. our silver cup, Plate 15, above), two Attic black glaze cups (Silantyeva 1959, 60–61, figs. 28–29) and a red-figure skyphos (ibid., 59, fig. 27). These objects, as well as the bronze mirror, ladle and sieve (ibid., 65–7, figs. 34–36) are all familiar from the contents of our grave groups, but we have nothing to match the Greek bronze candelabrum surmounted by an Ionic column and a statuette of a young athlete (ibid., 62–3). For all its wealth this grave serves to show how representative the inventories of the Ashmolean grave-groups are. Like them, it shows how a Scythian of some means has acquired a taste for Greek fashions while continuing to possess his own native artefacts. It has also been established beyond any reasonable doubt that the necropolis in which all these graves were found was that of the city of Nymphaeum itself (cf. Scholl and Zin'ko 1999, Maps 1–3, O3/O6), which implies that the Greek colonists and the native Scythians had achieved a high degree of assimilation (Silantyeva 1959, 51) by c.400 BC.

But who were the Scythians, and what were Greeks doing in Nymphaeum at all? The Scythians seem to have had their own origins as nomads in Central Asia, but by classical times they had moved into the steppes to the north of the Crimea and occupied the area roughly between Kiev on the Dnieper in the West and the Kuban region in the

East. Their distinctive 'animal style' art is of a kind which is widespread in Central Asia as far east as Kazakhstan and Siberia (Taylor 1996), but on coming into contact first with the civilisations of the Near East and then the Greek world, they adopted motifs from these areas and by the fifth and fourth centuries BC seem to have Greek craftsmen – or craftsmen trained *à la grecque* – working for them. There were Greek settlements on the north shores of the Black Sea from the later seventh century BC onwards, the colonists being attracted by the rich supplies of slaves (Taylor 2001*a*; 2001*b*), grain, cattle and salt fish that were available in the area. Nymphaeum was just one of these settlements, founded from Miletus in the mid-sixth century BC on the site of a Milesian trading post; by the later fifth century, it was a member of the Athenian empire. Its territory stretched for some kilometres inland, as the recent work of the Polish-Russian- Ukrainian team who worked on 'Project Nymphaion' has shown (Scholl and Zin'ko 1999). The Scythians provided the slaves and produce which were sent to mainland Greece and the Greek colonies in Asia Minor, and in exchange the Greeks supplied the Scythians with luxury articles, often far more elaborate than those we have been discussing. These might include weapons, silver-gilt vessels (cf. Vickers 1999*a*), and jewellery.

A stunning example of the latter was discovered in 1971 in a tumulus at Tolstaya mogila in the Ukraine (*From the Lands of the Scythians*, pls. 31–33, No.171; *Or des Scythes*, No. 70; Galanina and Grach 1986, 95–8, figs 118–21) in the form of a crescent-shaped gold pectoral, rather more than a kilo in weight, with three zones of ornament, the central one largely floral, but the inner and outer zones adorned with numerous small figures. In the outer zone are scenes of animals in combat, griffins attacking horses in the centre and panthers and lions attacking a stag and a boar on either side. The creatures then diminish in size through hounds and hares to pairs of grasshoppers in the corners. The inner zone is, if anything, even more interesting, for it gives us an insight into the life of Scythian nomads that is lacking even in Herodotus's vivid account (Book 4, 1–143). Here we see Scythians 'at home': dressing a fleece, and tending their animals: horses, cattle, sheep, goats, a pig, and a couple of birds. Great prominence is given to horses in this masterpiece of the jeweller's art, but this is what we might expect given the Scythians' dependence on horses for transport, milk (and koumiss), and food. We might remember the skeleton of a horse found in the tumulus in which our Grave I was situated, or the eight horses in the grander burial described above. They would have been slaughtered at the funeral, and Herodotus tells us that as many as fifty horses – and fifty slaves – might be killed at a royal funeral (Book 4, 72). Our grave goods are less distinguished, but are treasures all the same; both for the intrinsic value of some of the pieces of jewellery, and because of what they can tell us about the Scythian way of life.

Plate 1

Helmet probably from Grave 1(a)

There are two pieces: the crown itself and a small peak rivetted on to the front. Along the top of the helmet from front to back are two raised parallel ridges with three parallel lines incised between them. The holes around the lower edge of the helmet served for the attachment of a lining, perhaps of felt, as well as a leather protection for the neck. The small triangular nicks on the sides recall those on Illyrian helmets, a type which found especially in Northern Greece and the Balkans. Here we have such an Illyrian helmet trimmed down and fitted with a peak. The cranium in Plate 1 below left fits in the helmet. The fact that the owner of the cranium had suffered a severe blow to the head (from which he had recovered) may account for his acquiring this helmet which is remarkably thick by ancient standards. An early report stated that the helmet was of gilt bronze, but an X-ray fluorescence examination has established that this was not the case.

AN 1885.464. H.: 14.5 cm; W.:17.5 cm; L.: 21.5cm. Lit.: Gardner 1884, 65–6, p1. 46.2; the substantial subsequent literature can be found in Chernenko 1970, 193–4, n. 7; *Treasures* 34, pl. 1a–c; Vickers 1987, 44, fig. 2.

Cranium from Grave 1(a) and mandible from Grave 1(b)

The cranium is that of a male aged between 25 and 35. The crack across the forehead could not have been the fatal blow, for it appears to have healed up during the warrior's lifetime. He also seems to have suffered from a deviated saeptum. The jawbone is that of an adult female, and confirms Lyutsenko's statement that Grave I was a double burial of a warrior and a woman.

(Cranium) 1973.21. Circumference: 51 cm. Lit.: Biller 1868, I; Lyutsenko 1870, 54; Gardner 1884, 64; *Treasures* 35, pl. 2c; Vickers 1987, 44, fig. 3. (Mandible) 1973.22. L.: 9 cm; W.: 10.7 cm. Lit.: Biller 1868, I; *Treasures* 35, pl. 2d.

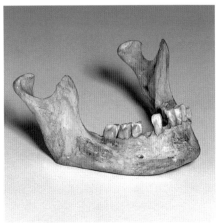

Plate 2

Arrowheads from Grave 1(a)

There are twenty-three arrowheads in all, twenty-two bronze and one bone. The shafts, of reeds, were extant when found, and fragments still remain in some of the sockets. The bronze examples are all triangular in form but fall into four different types which have been distinguished by Chernenko: (1) arrowheads with hollow sockets and with grooves as far as the tip; (2) socketed arrowheads with convex ribs and with grooves cut on three sides; (3) socketed arrowheads with the ends of the barbs shorn off with longer sockets and grooves to the tip; (4) socketed arrowheads with convex ribs, with barbs which extend beyond the socket and are marked with an oblique cross. All types are common in finds of arrowheads in the Northern Black Sea area.

AN 1885.467. L. (of longest): 4 cm; (of shortest): 2.7 cm. Lit.: Lyutsenko 1870, 54; Gardner 1884, 65, 68, pl. 46.5; Chernenko 1970, 198; *Treasures* 34, pl. 2a–b. On Scythian arrowheads in general, see Chernenko 1981, 94–110.

Plate 3

Pair of gold boat-shaped earrings from Grave 1(b)
These boat-shaped earrings terminate with the heads of
griffins. The 'boats' are decorated with bands of wire
(including double rows of twisted wire to give the illusion of cable patterns) and groups of granules arranged
in triangles. The point where the 'tail' is attached is in
the form of a rosette. Both are hollow and are made up
from several pieces: the 'leeches' in two parts, the join
disguised by means of the gold wire above and below.
The griffin heads too were made in two parts, and such
features as the ears, tongues and the knobs on the fore-
heads would have been added. This was a highly appro-
priate motif for Scythian gold work, for griffins were the
legendary guardians of the Central Asiatic gold-fields.
Boat-shaped earrings are very common in Scythian
graves: a pair sold at Sotheby's in 1871 (*Sale Catalogue*
24 June, Lot 237) now in the National Museum, Copenhagen (mv. 472) may well come from excavations at
Nymphaeum as well.

AN 1885.468. H.: 6 cm. Lit.: Lyutsenko 1870, 54; Gardner 1884, 68,
p1. 46.6 ('cocks'); Hadaczek 1903, 22, fig. 42; Rostovtzeff 1922, 79,
p1. 16.2; Becatti 1955, No. 293a–b, p1. 75 ('cocks'); Higgins 1961, 122,
p1. 24g; *Treasures* 35, pl. 3a.

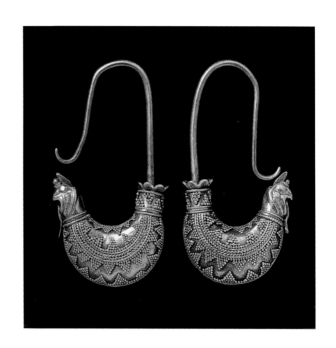

Plate 4

Attic red-figure pottery squat lekythos from Grave 1(b)

Two fawns seated on either side of a tree (the surface has flaked off so that only one deer is properly visible). Lyutsenko speaks of three clay lekythoi with painted decoration, and Biller a single pottery 'tearjug' with drawings on it, but 'wholly destroyed and decomposed'; it looks as though this is the sole survivor of the decorated wares from Grave 1(b). The shape and decoration belong in the late fifth century BC, which is the probable date of the burials in Grave 1. Squat lekythoi have been found in other graves at Nymphaeum, and also in tombs in Athens itself. Such vessels evoked silver ones decorated with gold-figure.

AN 1885.500 (V.538). H.: 10 cm; D.:5.6 cm. Lit.: Biller 1868, I; Lyutsenko 1870, 54; Lyutsenko 1869, 3; Gardner 1884, 65; P. Gardner 1884, 71; *CVA* Oxford i, pl. 40.20; *Treasures* 36, pl. 4a. Squat lekythoi at Nymphaeum: Silantyeva 1959, 33, fig. 11; on the Taman peninsula: Morgan 1999; at Pichvnari in Georgia: Vickers and Kakhidze 2001; their chronology: Sparkes and Talcott 1970, 1534. Gold-figure silver: Vickers 1999a. For deer as an element in the Scythian diet, see the discussion of Plate 5.

Bronze mirror from Grave 1(b)

Plain, except for a small volute near the handle (which is missing). This is a small version of a class of mirror that was exported in a luxury edition from Athens to Southern Russia in the fifth and fourth centuries BC. These often had the volute decoration at the handle enhanced with the addition of gold leaf. The reflecting surface would have consisted of a plating of tin (which is less prone to tarnishing than silver).

AN 1885.488. D.: 10.6 cm. Lit.: Biller 1868, I; Lyutsenko 1870, 54; Gardner 1884, 65; *Treasures* 36, pl. 3b.

Plate 5

Eighty-four gold hare appliqués from Grave 1(b)
Originally sewn on to the woman's dress by means of eyelets soldered on to the backs (now lost). Most gold appliqués which usually have holes pierced in them (cf. the lions in Plate 13). There is a vast range of subject matter on such appliqués; some are stylised in the Scythian manner, while others are relatively realistic. Greek coin types may underlie some of the latter variety. Appliqués were made over bronze matrices. Twenty-one hare appliqués similar to ours were found in a kurgan at Mgar near Poltava, Ukraine in 1989.

Hares often occur on artefacts found in Scythian tombs (cf. the *askos* in Plate 8), and hares were a standard item in the Scythian diet: animal bones from the Eastern Crimea show that hares were eaten, as well as cattle, horses, sheep, pigs and deer. A hare supposedly played a crucial role in the Scythians' relations with the Persians in 519/513 BC. Herodotus (Book 4, 134) tells how King Darius was frustrated at not being able to bring his Scythian opponents to battle. Eventually they did draw up in battle array, but 'it chanced that a hare started up between them and the Persians, and began running; at which all the Scythians who saw it immediately rushed off in pursuit, with great confusion and loud whoops and shouts'. Darius felt humiliated, gave up the attempt to conquer the Scythians, and turned back.

AN 1885.469. L.: 1.1 cm. Lit.: Biller 1868, I; Lyutsenko 1870, 54; Gardner 1884, 68–9, pl. 46.7; *Treasures* 36–7, pl.4b–c; Vickers 1987, 45, fig. 4. Appliqués on trouser legs: *From the Lands of the Scythians* No. 72; *Or des Scythes* No. 66; on women's hoods: Miroshina 1977, 79–94. Mgar kurgan: Kulatova and Suprunenko 1996, 325, 331, fig. 14, 333, fig. 17, 337, nn. 9–12 (with bibliography); Greek coin types with hares: Cesano 1937, 89–94. Matrix: Shramko 1970. Hares in the Scythian diet; Bibikova, 1970, 97.

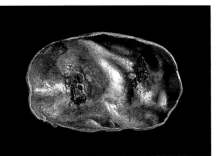
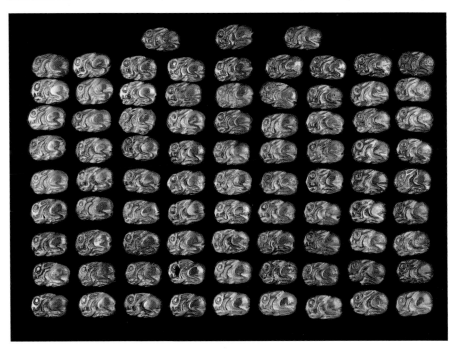

Plate 6

Textile fragments from Grave 1(b)
The textile fragments from Nymphaeum have been
divided into two sorts: Textile 1. A fine wool textile in
plain weave, now dark brown in colour and brittle.
About 9 cm^2 of it survive, but there are no selvedges.
System 1 (the warp) is widespread, at c. 14 threads per
cm and System 2 (the weft) rather closer together, at c.
60–70 threads per cm. Textile 2. A mass of loose strands
of yarn, mostly dark brown and purple-brown, though
some are apparently black and dark green, which may
be due to discoloration rather than dye. The strands are
identical with System 1 of Textile 1 but there is no trace
of another system. If one did exist, it may have been of
very fine yarn of vegetable origin. There are also some
pieces of cord. The fibre has been analysed by Dr M.L.
Ryder and has proved to be of wool, spun from the
fleece of a fine-wool sheep, and is much the earliest
example of this fleece-type. The suggestion has been
made that the textiles were imports from Miletus, Milesian fine-wool sheep being famous in antiquity, and
trading links between Miletus and the Black Sea being
particularly close. Nymphaeum, indeed, was a Milesian
colony.

AN 1885.475–478. Lit.: Biller 1868, I; Lyutsenko 1870, 54; Ryder and
Hedges 1973, 480; Wild 1978, 334; *Treasures* 37, pl. 5a–b; Vickers
1999*b*, 32, 66, fig. 19.

25

Plate 7

Necklace of gold rams' heads from Grave 2

Twenty-six more or less identical pieces, each made in two halves, the sheet metal being impressed into a mould. The joins are quite visible in most cases. The eyes were added later as was a triangular patch of granulation on the forehead.

AN 1885.493. L. (of each head): 1.5 cm. Lit.: Biller 1868, II; Gardner 1884, 65, 72, p1. 47.12; *Treasures* 38, pl. 6a. For granulation techniques see Nestler and Formigli 1993; Platz-Horster 2001, 38–40.

Gold ring with sphinx from Grave 2

An intaglio of a crouching winged sphinx on a hatched exergue; in the corners, sprigs of olive. The style of the decoration on the bezel, and the form of the ring (stirrup-shaped with a flat, slim, leaf-shaped bezel) point to a date of the second quarter of the fifth century. It has been attributed to 'the Penelope Group'. Of the five gems in this group three have South Russian provenances, and one, of a flying Nike with a wreath, also comes from Nymphaeum.

AN 1885.492. L. (of bezel): 1.7cm. Lit.: Biller 1868, II; Lyutsenko 1869, 1; Gardner 1884, 65, 72, p1. 47.11; Boardman 1970, 215,296, p1. 657; Taylor and Scarisbrick 1978, 34, No. 59; Boardman and Vollenweider 1978, 30, p1. 23, No.129; *Treasures* 38, fig. 3, pl. 6b–c; Vickers 1987, 45, fig. 6.

Gold earrings from Grave 2

These unusual objects were found at the shoulders of the deceased, and were assumed in the past to have served as dress fasteners. Each ring was made in two halves, which were decorated and joined together along their sides. The actual fasteners are at the ends which interlock with pairs of eyelets on the tips of the penannular rings. The rings are very flimsy and cannot have held much weight. A more recent suggestion that they are earrings is to be preferred.

AN 1885.494. D.:4.2–4.8 cm. Lit.: Biller 1868, II, Gardner 1884, 65, 72, p1. 47.13; *Treasures* 38, pl. 6d; Williams and Ogden 1994, 134.

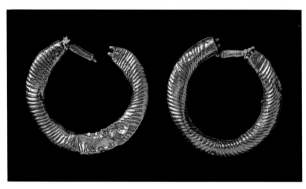

Plate 8

Attic red-figure pottery askos from Grave 2

On one side, a satyr pours wine into a drinking horn from an amphora, and on the other another a satyr crawls towards him extending his drinking horn. Beazley dated this *askos* to *c.* 430 BC. Satyrs were regarded as behaving in ways which transgressed normal rules of conduct. Crawling and crouching were considered ungentlemanly in Greek terms: squatting was completely undignified and suitable only for slaves. And no self-respecting Greek would drink his wine neat or without its being strained. Drinking horns were characteristic Scythian, Thracian, Macedonian and Persian vessels; gold specimens have survived in burials.

AN 1885.499 (V.541). H.: 6.5 cm; D.:8.8 cm. Lit.: Lyutsenko 1869, 4; Gardner 1884, 65; *CVA* Oxford i, p1. 45.2; Hoffmann 1977, 6, 12, No. La2; *Treasures* 38–9, fig. 4, pl. 7a–b; Vickers 1987, 46, fig. 10. Squatting a shameful posture: Himmelmann 1971, 36. Drinking horns in Scythian art: *From the Lands of the Scythians*, Nos. 72, 74, 76, 79; *Or des Scythes*, Nos. 66a, 96–97, 105; *Gold und Kunsthandwerk*, 121, pls. 18–19, No. 100.

Attic red-figure pottery askos from Grave 2

The motif of a hound chasing a hare is a common one in Scythian art, and was too, presumably, in Scythian life. There are hounds chasing hares on the pectoral from Tolstaya mogila and elsewhere, and it seems possible that *askoi* such as this, whether in gold-figure silverware, or in simple pottery, were designed specifically for the Scythian market. Beazley dated it to the late fifth century.

AN 1885.498 (V.542). H.: 6.9 cm; D.:8.8 cm. Lit.: Lyutsenko 1869, 4; Gardner 1884, 65; P. Gardner 1884, 73; *CVA* Oxford i, p1. 45.4; Beazley 1963, 964.9; Hoffmann, 11, No. Aa7 (add an *askos* from tumulus VI of the Seven Brothers Barrows in Kuban with a lion chasing a hare, *Compte Rendu de la Commission Archéologique Impériale* 1876, 130–31); *Treasures* 39, fig. 5, pl. 8a; Vickers 1987, 46, fig. 9.

Plate 9

Attic black-gloss pottery stemless cup from Grave 2

A stoutly made pottery drinking vessel with an offset lip. The side of the foot is lipped and reserved (i.e. is not black). The underside is reserved and has a black dot and circle in the middle. There is a graffito Achaxe, probably an owner's name, written in Ionian letters beneath. Several similar cups of equally massive proportions (including one bearing the Greek graffito 'I am the cup [kylix] of Euthymias': Silantyeva 43, fig. 20) have been found at Nymphaeum. Some maintain that sturdy cups like these (now generally called Castulo cups after a site in Spain which produced many pieces) were best suited to long-distance travel (their distribution extends as far as the Atlantic coast of Spain, taking in Sardinia, Magna Graecia and Sicily, Rhodes and Palestine, as well as the Black Sea [one has been found as far east as Aksyutintsy, 170 km east of Kiev]); others would see them as ceramic versions of heavy silver vessels. They used to be dated to the first half of the fifth century BC, but it now seems that they were made well into the second half. This makes sense in the present context, for all the other pottery from Grave II was certainly made in the second half of the fifth century.

AN 1885.495. H.: 7.5 cm; D.: 21.2 cm. Lit.: Biller 1868, II; Gardner 1884, 65; CVA Oxford i, p1. 48.2; Sparkes and Talcott 1970, 268, No. 470; Treasures 40, fig. 7, pl. 9a–b; Vickers 1987, 46, fig. 7; Shefton 1996, 174, pl. 2a–b. Aksyutintsy cup: Onaiko 1966, 61–2, No. 168, pl. 9.9. The name Achaxe is not referred to by Zgusta 1955, but it has recently been re-published in Nawotka 2000.

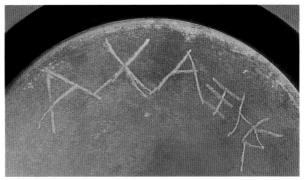

Plate 10

Attic black-gloss cosmetic box [*lekanis*] from Grave 2

Elegantly turned *lekanides* of this type are called Lykinic after the graffito found on the lid of one example. This example has a deep bowl, wishbone handles and an unusual knob which is reserved on top and decorated with concentric circles. Parallels found in the Athenian Agora have been dated to 430–420 BC, which is probably when this was made.

AN 1885.496. H.: 10.8 cm; D.:12.2 cm. Lit.: Biller 1868, II, Gardner 1884, 65; *CVA* Oxford p1. 48.19; Sparkes and Talcott 1970, 168–70; *Treasures* 40–1, fig. 8, pl. 9c.

Attic black-gloss pottery cup-*skyphos* from Grave 2

The pot is delicately made. The bowl has a single curve, the upper side of the foot is convex, and the foot is black underneath. Probably to be dated to the end of the fifth century BC. The thin glaze is badly fired.

AN 1885.497. H.: 5.6 cm; D.: 10.8 cm. Lit.: Biller 1868, II; Gardner 1884, 65, *CVA* Oxford i, p1. 48.3. Cf. Sparkes and Talcott 1970, 273, No. 539 (of *c.* 420 BC); *Treasures* 39, fig. 6, pl. 8b.

Plate 11

Electrum necklace from Grave 3

Consists of twenty-five units, each made from a rectangle of sheet metal from which a fluted or knobbed bead is suspended. Eight of the rectangular plates are larger than the others and bear rosettes of gold wire (some have two beads suspended from them). As reconstructed, these plates alternate with the regular ones at the centre of the necklace. Part of the fastener is preserved: a trapezoidal piece of folded metal which provides the mooring for a pair of threads the correct distance apart to carry the rectangular plates. Electrum is an alloy of gold and silver.

AN 1885.502. L.: 25 cm. Lit.: Biller 1868, III; Gardner 1884, 66, 71–2, pl. 47.9; Becatti 1955, No. 425, pl. 115; Higgins 1961, 129, pl. 27a; *Treasures* 41, pl. 10a; Vickers 1987, 47, fig. 11.

Silver and electrum bracelets from Grave 3

The finials are in the form of lions' heads, done in electrum. Their worn condition enables us to see how they were constructed: the heads were each made from two pieces of sheet metal, and the necks from a strip of electrum mounted with pieces of twisted wire laid side by side. Normally this creates the illusion of a cable pattern, but twice here the wires have been carelessly laid and can be seen for what they are. The lions' heads closely resemble those on the finials of a gold torc found in a Scythian tomb at Kakhovka in 1969. The penannular form of these bracelets recalls that of Achaemenid Persian bracelets.

AN 1885.503. D.: 7.4 cm. Lit.: Biller 1868, III; Lyutsenko 1869, 5; Gardner 1884, 66, 72, pl. 47.10; *Treasures* 41, pl. 10b; Vickers 1987, 47, fig. 11. Kakhovka torc: Leskov 1974, 73, fig. 103.

Plate 12

Gold necklace from Grave 4

There are few more exquisite pieces of jewellery from
the classical period than this necklace. Twenty-two
rosettes with acorns suspended from them alternate
with stylised lotuses which support small beads. Both
rosettes and lotuses each have another, much smaller,
rosette attached to them. All these elements are made of
sheet gold edged with beaded gold wire. They may well
have once been enamelled. A letter from Sir William
Siemens of November 1880 refers to the fact that 'the
gold [of the acorn necklace] was rubbed to show the
effect, whereas all the other ornaments have been left
just in the condition in which they were found'. A necklace from Panticapaeum of equivalent delicacy still
retains its (pastel blue) enamel.

AN 1885.482. L. (as strung): 31 cm. Lit.: Biller 1868, IV; Lyutsenko
1869, 1; Gardner 1884, 66, 70, pl. 47.4; Rostovtzeff 1922, pl. 16.4;
Becatti 1955, No. 426, pl. 115; P. Coche de la Ferté 1956, pl. 20.2; Higgins 1961, 129, pl. 27a; *Treasures* 41–2, pl. 11a–b. Panticapaeum
necklace: Williams and Ogden 1994, 152–3, No. 94.

Earrings from Grave 4

Made of bronze with an electrum casing and terminals.
These last consist of pyramids of granules and collar
ornaments of wire figure-of-eight spirals with granules
in the loops. Biller took them to be clothes fasteners, but
fifth-century Lycian coins show similar earrings being
worn in large holes in the earlobe.

AN 1885.483. H.: 3.5 cm. Lit.: Biller 1868, IV; Gardner 1884, 66,
70–71, pl. 47.5; Rostovtzeff 1922, pl. 16.3; Becatti 1955, No. 378, pl.
99; Higgins 1961, 123, pl. 24f; *Treasures* 42, pl. 11c. See discussions
in: Williams and Ogden 1994, 95, No. 47; Platz-Horster 2001, 55–6,
No. 33.

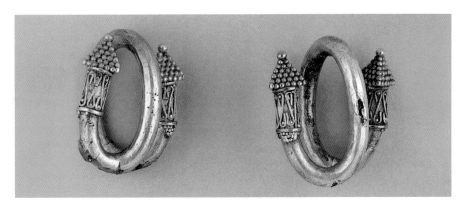

Plate 13

Forty-nine gold lion appliqués from Grave 4
These lions, like the hares above (Plate 5), would have been sewn on to a garment, but unlike them have holes pierced in them for this purpose. In this respect they resemble the majority of appliqués from Scythian graves. Although they are done in a summary fashion these lions are in no way stylised. Rather, they appear realistically alert and ready to pounce on their prey.

AN 1885.480. L. (of each): 1.3 cm. Lit.: Biller 1868, IV; Gardner 1884, 70, pl. 47.3; *Treasures* 42, pl. 12a–b; Vickers 1987, 47, fig. 13.

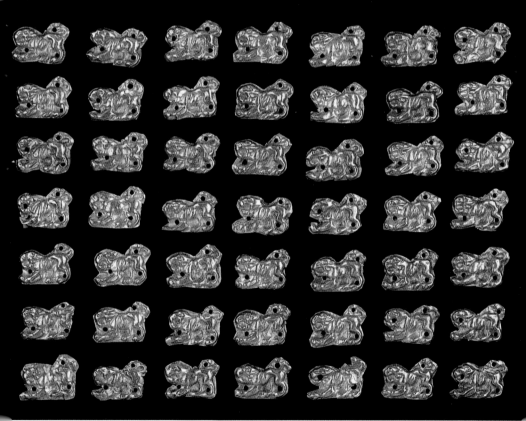

Plate 14

Bronze strainer from Grave 4

Such strainers, with a sieve in the centre and a duck's head handle, were very common in the Greek world, and many have survived. They were, after all, part of any respectable drinker's equipment, for wine straight from the amphora would have contained impurities. A strainer of this kind can be seen suspended (together with a ladle) on a pottery cup in New York.

AN 1885.487. L.: 24.6 cm; D.:11.8 cm. Lit.: Biller 1868, IV; Lyutsenko 1869, 7; Gardner 1884, 66; *Treasures* 43–4, pl. 16a. New York cup: Mertens 1976, 74–5, fig. 7.

Bronze libation bowl (*patera*) handle from Grave 4

The way in which the junction point is curved shows it came from a bowl, rather than a mirror. Handles of this type, with a thumb rest on the upper surface, volute and palmette decorations, and an ornate suspension hole, are thought to be Etruscan in origin; cf. a similar handle on a wine strainer from Melfi in Southern Italy.

AN 1885.470a. L.: 18 cm. Lit.: Biller 1868, IV; Gardner 1884, 69, p1. 46.9; Jacobsthal and Langsdorf 1929, 46–7, n. 6; Kunze 1951, 743, n. 29; Bilimovich 1978, 33, n. 43; *Treasures* 43, pl. 13b–c. Melfi strainer: Hermann 1966, 317, figs. 82–83.

Bronze mirror disc from Grave 4

This mirror disc has been associated with the patera handle above, but this is unlikely. Instead, the handle was probably made of another material – wood, bone, ivory or iron – which has disintegrated or corroded away.

AN 1885.470b. D.: 17.5 cm. Lit.: Biller 1868, IV; Gardner 1884, 69; *Treasures* 43, pl. 13d

Plate 15

Silver cup from Grave 4

One of the very few pieces of plate to have survived from the late fifth century BC; most have gone into the melting pot. The bowl was hammered out from a disc of silver; the lip was tooled inside and out and the underside decorated with three concentric tooled ridges on a lathe. The handles and foot were cast separately and soldered on. The only close parallel in silver comes from Vouni in Cyprus, but similar shapes exist in the derivative black-gloss pottery of the late fifth century, and there is a bronze example in the National Museum in Copenhagen. A silver cup of the third quarter of the fourth century was found at Taman on the Kuban peninsula. The silver is extremely pure (98.7%; analysis Dr S.Stos), and its weight is equivalent to 33.33 Persian silver coins.

AN 1885.486. H.: 5.6 cm; D.: 10.5 cm; W.: 16.2 cm; Wt. : 183.31 g. Lit.: Biller 1868, IV; Gardner 1884, 66; Strong 1966, 85, p1. 17a; Sparkes and Talcott 1970, 111, n. 21; Oliver 1977, 31, No. 6; *Treasures* 42–3, fig. 9, pl. 13a; Gill 1986, 15, 18, fig.16; Vickers, Impey and Allan 1986, pl. 3a; Vickers 1987, 48, fig. 14; Vickers and Gill (1996) 119, fig. 5.13; Vickers 1999a, 8, pl. 2.3. Vouni cup: Gjerstad *et al.* 1937, 238, 274, No. 292d, pls. 90, 92. Taman cup: Pharmakowsky 1913, 181–5, fig. 13.

Chalcedony scaraboid from Grave 5

This ferocious-looking winged horned lion belongs to the Achaemenid menagerie of mythological beasts, and serves as a reminder of the close links the Scythians had with Persia. It belongs to a class of gems known as 'Greco-Persian' which were made in the later fifth and fourth centuries BC by Greek craftsmen for Persian clients. Many have been found in Scythian graves, but few are as grand as this example.

AN 1885.491. H.: 2.7cm. W.: 2cm. Lit.: Biller 1868, V; Lyutsenko 1869, 9; Gardner 1884, 66–71, pl. 47.8; Furtwängler 1900, pl. 12.4; Rostovtzeff 1922, pl. 16.1; Lippold 1922, pl. 81.2; Boardman 1970, pl. 838; *Treasures* 44, pl. 14b–c; Vickers 1987, 48, fig. 16. For numerous Graeco-Persian gems from Scythian contexts: Minns 1913, 411, fig. 298.

Plate 16

Bronze elk's head plaque from Grave 6

This impressive elk's head is the only major piece of characteristically Scythian artistry amongst the finds from Nymphaeum in Oxford. It has a pendulous lower lip and a huge over-hanging nose, summary nostrils and a large staring eye surrounded by deeply incised lids. The ears and mane are also incised. The horn is as small as the nose is large, in keeping with the highly stylised nature of the object; indeed, the horn terminates in the form of a stylised bird's head. On the back is a small bracket with which it was attached to the breastplate. It seems likely, at least, that this was the case, although as Chernenko notes, the ten or so similar elks' head plaques found in other Scythian graves were not actually recorded in *situ*. Two more elks' head plaques have been found at Nymphaeum, as well as lions' head plaques made in a very similar manner. This style, the 'animal style', was extremely widespread in Asia, and related artefacts have been found as far as Mongolia, and even beyond.

AN 1885.466.H.: 8.3 cm; W.: 11.6cm. Lit. : Lyutsenko 1870, 55; Lyutsenko 1869, 2; Gardner 1884, 67–8, pl. 46.4 ('camel'); Rostovtzeff 1929, pl. 10.7; Talbot Rice 1957, pl. 44; Portratz 1963, pl. 77; Chernenko 1970, 194–5, fig. 3; *Treasures* 44, 16a. Elks' and lions' head plaques from Nymphaeum: Silantyeva, 84–5, figs. 474–8.

Plate 17

Fragment of scale armour from Grave 6

Part of the leather cuirass reported by Lyutsenko from Grave VI. It once had eleven rows of bronze plates sewn on to a double leather backing by means of rawhide thongs, and the whole is surrounded by a leather strip. Judging by a similar fragment in a tumulus at Volkovtsy, it was one of the epaulettes of the cuirass. Dr R. Reed has identified this object as being principally made of sheep- or goat-skin; the edging is probably of calf-skin.

AN 1885.465. L.: 22.5 cm: W.:13 cm. Lit.: Lyutsenko 1870, 55; Gardner 1884, 67, pl. 46.3; Chernenko 1970, 1934, fig. 2; *Treasures* 45, pl. 15b–c; Vickers 1987, 49, fig. 17. Volkovtsy tumulus: Chernenko 1965, 150, figs. 6–7.

Bronze and leather greave from Grave 6

This greave is but one of the pair mentioned by Lyutsenko in his description of Grave VI. It consists of thirteen long, overlapping, rectangular bronze strips attached by means of bronze wire to a backing of sheep- or goat-skin, the whole edged in calf-skin (identifications by Dr R. Reed, of the Procter Department of Food and Leather Science at he University of Leeds). There are no traces of any arrangements for attaching the greave to the ankle, and it may have been pushed into a boot or a sock like a footballer's shin-pad. The indentation at the bottom was clearly intended to fit over the foot.

AN 1885.463. L.: 20.4 cm. Lit.: Lyutsenko 1870, 55; Gardner 1884, 66, p1. 46.1; Chernenko 1970, 195–7, fig. 4; *Treasures* 45, pl. 16b.

Plate 18

Electrum torc from Grave 6

Neck decorations such as this are fairly common in Scythian burials, but some are more elaborate. One with lions' head terminals like those on our silver bracelets (pl. 11) was found at Kakhovka, and the most elaborate of all, from Kul Oba near Kerch, has a pair of Scythian riders astride each end.

AN 1885.472. D.:17.5 cm; Wt.: 165 g; Lit.: Lyutsenko 1870, 55; Gardner 1884, 65; *Treasures* 44, pl. 15a. Kakhovka torc: Leskov 1974, 73, fig. 103; Kul Oba torc: *From the Lands of the Scythians*, No. 83; *Or des Scythes*, No. 92; Galanina and Grach 1986, 101, figs 126–7; Williams and Ogden 1994, 137, No. 81.

Gold ring with bearded man

Much worn, but we can still see the features of a middle-aged man with high cheek bones, an aquiline nose, short hair and a stubbly beard; perhaps a portrait of a specific individual. This is a rare phenomenon in the second half of the fifth century BC, but cf. the similar, but better preserved, ring bearing a portrait in Berlin, or the striking jasper scaraboid in Boston with the portrait of another bearded man and signed by the gem cutter Dexamenos.

AN 1885.484. L. (of bezel): 1.4 cm. Lit.: Lyutsenko 1869, 1; Gardner 1884, 66, 71, pl. 47.6; Beazley 1920, 48, pl. A.29; Jacobsthal 1931, 56, fig. 35; Richter 1961–62, 56–7, fig. 25; Richter 1968, No. 325; Boardman 1970, 296, pl. 670; Metzler 1971, 311, fig. 26; Taylor and Scarisbrick 1978, 34, No. 60; Boardman and Vollenweider 1978, 30, pl. 23, No. 131; *Treasures* 46, pl. 17b–c; Vickers 1987, 48, fig. 15. The Berlin ring: Platz-Horster 2001, 54–5, No. 32; the Boston gem: Boardman 1970, pl. 466.

Gold ring with a facing head

A youth with *wings* on his head, or are they *horns* like those of river gods? The cicada above his head may refer to the Greek word for both a cicada and a male hair ornament (*tettix*). Such oval bezels are prevalent in the fourth century BC.

AN 1885.490. L (of bezel): 1.6 cm. Lit.: Gardner 1884, 66, 71, pl. 47.7; Richter, No. 317 ('wings'); Boardman 1970, 223, 299, pl. 730 ('horns'); Taylor and Scarisbrick 1978, 35, No. 71; Boardman and Vollenweider 1978, 31, pl. 25, No. 135; *Treasures* 46, 17d–e.

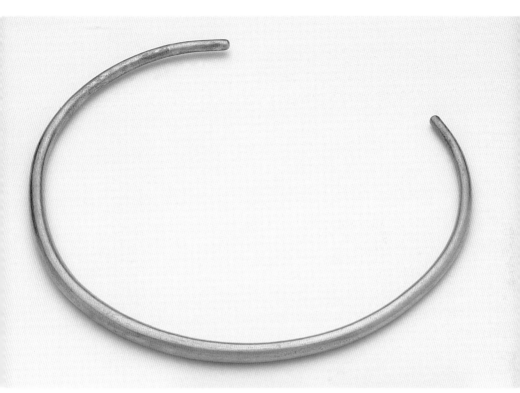

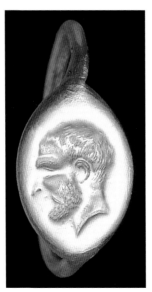

Plate 19

Bronze ladle from Grave 6

This ladle has a fairly shallow bowl, a stem which is square in section, and a goose- head terminal. And it is without doubt a goose's head, rather than the duck's head that is more customary in such contexts (cf. the duck's head on the strainer from Grave IV [Plate 14]). It has the characteristic beak of a goose and the eyes and neck-feathers are clearly shown. Ladles were part of the standard equipment for the symposium, where they were regularly used for dispensing wine from the mixing bowl into drinking cups (like those in Plates 10, 15, or 28). The form of our ladle is what we might expect towards the end of the fifth century BC. Earlier in the century, the bowl was deep and egg-shaped, and by the late fourth century it had become lower and wider, shallower even than ours. The handles are flat by this time and often have decorative volutes at the point where the bowl and handle meet.

AN 1885.473. L.: 34.5 cm. Lit.: Lyutsenko 1870, 55; Lyutsenko 1869, 6; Gardner 1884, 65; *Treasures* pl. 17a. For ladles, their use and development: Mertens 1976 71–8, and Vickers 1981, 557–8, fig. 20.

Glass alabastron

This alabastron is a fifth-century version of a well-known type of vessel made on a core, perhaps of clay (but not of sand). Molten glass was wound around the core and smoothed ('marvered') on a flat stone slab before being combed into festoons or zig-zags, as here. The colours of this piece – light blue, brown and yellow – are slightly unusual. The place of manufacture is unknown, and it is unlikely that all such core-made vessels were made only in Syria, as is often supposed, and it has been suggested that workshops may have been set up in the Aegean or perhaps in Cyprus. Other glass alabastra have been found at Nymphaeum, and elsewhere in the Black Sea, notably at Pichvnari.

AN 1885.501. H.: 10.6 cm. Lit.: Gardner 1884, 65; Fossing 1940, 68, fig. 42; *Treasures* 47, pl. 17f; Vickers 1987, 50, fig. 19; Newby 2001, 12–13, No. 3. On core-made glass in general: Harden 1968, 50, 53–5, fig. 3; Grose 1989. Alabastra at Nymphaeum: Silantyeva, 24, fig. 8; at Pichvnari: Vickers and Kakhidze 2001.

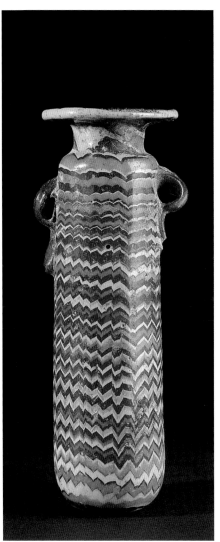

Plate 20

Pair of bracelets with rams' head terminals

The bracelets have a bronze core, but are encased in gold. The terminals are in the form of rams' heads, each made in two pieces joined down the centre. The collars decorated with spirals of gold wire recall the anthemion bands of Ionic architectural decoration (e.g. on the Erechtheum at Athens). Like the lion's head bracelets (Plate 11) their form is akin to that of Achaemenid bracelets. We do not know to which grave group these bracelets belong, but it is most likely that they came from Grave IV which contained the rich necklace (Plate 12, above) and the hair ornaments (Plate 12, below) with their similar collar ornament.

AN 1885.479. D.: 8.5 cm. Lit.: Lyutsenko 1869, 5; Gardner 1884, 66, 69, pl. 47.1; Becatti 1955, no. 370, p1. 95; *Treasures* pl. 18e; Vickers 1987, 49, fig. 18.

Electrum ring

This ring could have come from Grave 1(b) or Grave V. It is of a form which is usual down to the middle of the fifth century BC. (Boardman 1970, 212–13, Type I).

AN 1885.474. W.:2.4 cm. Lit.: Biller 1868, I/V; Lyutsenko 1870, 54; Fig. 12 2:1 Gardner 1884, 65–6; *Treasures* pl. 18a *top*, fig. 12.

Electrum ring

Again the grave from which this ring came is uncertain: Grave 1(b) or Grave V. (Boardman 1970, 212–14, Type II).

AN 1885.485. W.: 2.2 cm. Lit.: Biller 1868 I/V; Lyutsenko 1870, 54; Gardner 1884, 65–6; *Treasures* pl. 18 a *bottom*.

Two electrum bosses

It is uncertain as to which grave these bosses belonged; equally uncertain is their precise function. They seem to have been attached to a garment. There seem to be no precise parallels in other Scythian graves.

AN 1885.471. D.:2.5 cm. Lit.: Gardner 1884, p1. 48.8; *Treasures* pl. 18d.

Female head gold appliqué

The long curly hair on this head argues for it representing a woman rather than a youth. The two holes are for sewing it to a garment, but there is no evidence as to which grave it was found in.

AN 1885.481. H.: 2 cm; W.:1.2 cm. Lit.: Gardner 1884, 69–70, p1. 47.2; *Treasures* pl. 18e.

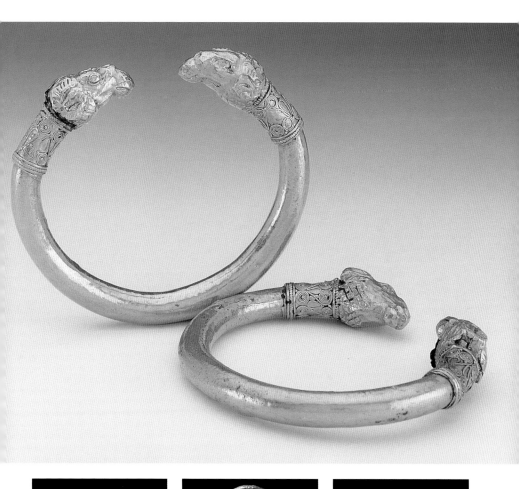

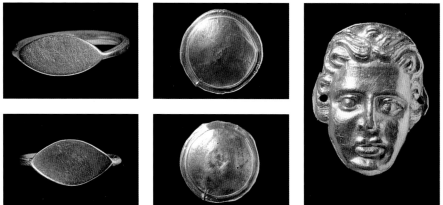

Plate 21

Gold appliqués

Left: Female head, wearing a *sakkos,* to right. It greatly resembles coins of Nymphaeum. From Kerch (Panticapaeum). Later 5th century BC.

AN 1910.95. D.: 1.5 cm. Gift of Sir Oliver Wardrop.

Centre: Stylised griffin to left, in rectangular frame. Later 5th or 4th century BC.

AN 1921.4. 2 x 1.8 cm. Bought from Count Alexis Bobrinskoy ('a relic of Prince Bobrinskoy's collection; picked up on the floor of his looted house').

Right: Forepart of a winged boar, a type known from coins of Greek Ialysos and Clazomenae. From Kul Oba.

AN 1953.49. H.: 2.1 W.: 2.4 cm. Bought.

'Ghost money'

Top row, left: Two gold foil discs impressed with a 4th century coin type of Panticapaeum: frontal Medusa head.

AN 1888.1529. D.: 1.6 cm, AN 1888.1532. D.: 1.5 cm. Bought at Kerch.

Top row, right: A gold foil disc impressed with a 4th century coin type of Panticapaeum: lion's head, to left, N.

AN 1888.1530. D.: 1.6 cm. Bought at Kerch.

Electrum foil disc impressed with the type of a coin of Pautalia (?).

AN 1888.1527. D.: 1.9 cm. Bought at Kerch.

Middle row: Gold foil discs reproducing the reverse of a bronze coin struck by Machares for his father Mithridates, 80–73 BC: Dionysiac herm, palm-branch, fillet and monogram.

AN 1888.1533. D.: 2.1 cm, AN 1888.1534. D.: 2.3 cm. Bought at Kerch.
AN 1910.93. D.: 2.3 cm, AN 1910.94. D.: 2 cm. Sir Oliver Wardrop gift.

Bottom, left: gold foil disc impressed with the type of a Roman denarius, perhaps Vespasian.

AN 1888.1528. D.: 1.7 cm. Bought at Kerch.

Bottom, right: gold foil disc; impressed with an uncertain coin type, probably post-classical.

AN 1888.1531. D.: 1.6 cm. Bought at Kerch.

Thracian antiquities

In 1879, Bulgaria was attempting to throw off the
Ottoman yoke, and resisted their Turkish rulers
with the help of Russian military assistance. In the
spring of that year a cemetery in the village of Dalboki, some miles east of Stara Zagora in north
central Bulgaria, was being cleared under the super-

vision of a Russian officer Sub-Lieut. N.P.Kliusov, and on 12 April an important Thracian burial came to light. Its rich contents included an electrum pectoral, silver drinking vessels, and bronze armour. Weather conditions at the time of the excavation were such that torrential rain disturbed the contents (Prochorov 1880, 2). A description of the grave and its contents was published in St Petersburg in the following year (Prochorov 1880). The objects were probably taken to St Petersburg, for a silver beaker belonging to the group is now in the Hermitage (D. 1403; acquired in 1880; Filov 1931–32, 51, fig. 39; Dimitrov 1950, 225–6, figs. 22–3; Grach 1985, 18–19, No. 8; Vickers and Gill 1996, 50, fig. 2.5). By 1908, however, the other contents of the tomb were in the Cook collection at Doughty House, Richmond (Strong 1908, 45, No. 81), and when this was dispersed in 1947, they came to the Ashmolean, having been presented by the Seven Pillars of Wisdom Trust in memory of T.E.Lawrence (Ashmolean 1948).

The grave consisted of a rectangular cist, 2.35 metres long, 1.60 m wide, and 1.50 m high, built of limestone slabs, and roofed in the same material. It lay two feet below ground surface, so that any original covering mound there may have been had entirely disappeared. The site today is in a gently rolling field. Inside the cist was found a male skele-

ton, head to the west, wearing a bronze cuirass, on which lay the gold pectoral. Around the body were many fragments of iron, taken by the excavator to be iron spears. At the feet were an iron lamp stand, four silver, three bronze and five clay vases, together with some of the wood from the coffin.

We are thus taken back into the world of the ancient Thracians, a numerous people, according to Herodotus, who sold their children into slavery abroad. Tattoos were admired, as was idleness; to be a 'tiller of the soil [was] a great dishonour'. They worshipped Ares, Dionysus and Artemis alone, but their kings claimed descent from Hermes. The rich were buried in the following fashion: 'They expose the body for three days; and when they have done lamenting, they slaughter all manner of beasts and feast upon them. Then they bury the body, sometimes burning it and sometimes not; and having raised a mound, they hold all kinds of contests, in which the greatest prizes are given for single combat. Thus the Thracians are buried.' (Book 5, 6–7).

Unlike Greece or Italy, it was common practice in Thrace to place objects of precious metal in aristocratic graves. At Athens, the question would not have arisen, for the rich were cremated, and in Etruria painted pottery was placed in tombs as a surrogate for the family silver which would remain above ground and be passed on to the next generation. The Thracians (like the Scythians) were notoriously careless of such considerations, and some of the finest extant Persian and Greek metalwork has been found in the lands to the north of the Aegean.

Recent research on ancient gold and silverware has suggested that great pains were taken to make objects, or sets of objects, conform to recognised weight standards; as Dr Dietrich von Bothmer has put it: 'the weights of gold and silver objects were usually rendered in units of a commonly used coin'. Plate in effect served as large denomination banknotes.

By far the most common was the Persian standard, and this seems to have been employed for the

Dalboki silver. This, however, only became clear when Russian colleagues supplied the weight of the beaker in the Hermitage. The total weight of the three beakers is 560 grams, equivalent to 100 Persian *sigloi* (the *siglos* was a coin whose ideal weight was 5.67 grams), and it is likely that they formed a set made by craftsmen of varying degrees of skill. One of the beakers is very carefully worked, the other two considerably less so. The mug weighs 60 *sigloi*.

The ancients preferred to have their silver as pure as possible. When Dr Sophie Stos analysed the Oxford vases by energy dispersive X-ray fluorescence the beakers proved to contain 98.5 and 99.4% silver, and the mug 98%. This contrasts with the 92.5% of today's sterling silver which usually has copper added to harden it. Pure silver is conversely very soft, and this may have inhibited regular cleaning in antiquity, for this would have led in both theory and practice to a reduction of the amount of silver and consequent impoverishment. In places by the sea, pure silver would achieve a rich dark patina, an effect which was probably admired, for it seems to have been imitated by potters with varying degrees of success. A photograph of the Dalboki silver taken soon after its arrival in Oxford in 1948 shows the beakers to have been shiny black, very similar to the effect achieved by the potter of one of the two Attic black-gloss stemless cups from the group, which can be dated to *c.* 430. This is the date of the latest objects in the tomb; others, notably the cuirass, are probably much earlier.

Plate 22

Gold pectoral

This semi-circular gold sheet pectoral was probably made for funerary purposes, both being too flimsy for daily (or even ceremonial) use, and bearing few signs of wear. There are moreover only two small holes (upper left and upper right) for suspension. It was, however, perhaps laid over a rather more substantial iron pectoral. Judging by the iron corrosion products still adhering to the left side of the front of the cuirass, and the presence of many corroded iron fragments when the tomb was opened, the gold panel may have been placed on top of an iron pectoral akin to the Thracian iron and silver collar-pectoral from Mezek. The Duvanli pectoral is semi-circular, with an indentation for the neck. All the decoration is impressed: tongue motifs, circles and beechnuts, and rows of rosettes and panther heads within and around the four segments into which the surface is divided. A score of pectorals is known from the Thracian region, but they vary considerably in size and shape.

AN 1948.96. H.: 22.9cm; W.: 35.5cm; Wt: 75 g. Lit.: Prochorov 1880, pls. 3.3, 4.1; Filov 1931–32, 47, 55 No. 1; Ashmolean 1948, 20, pl. 2; Dimitrov 1950, 214–6, fig. 7, No. 2; *Thracian Treasures* 93–5, No. 548. Mezek collar-pectoral: Danov and Ivanov 1980, 25–6.

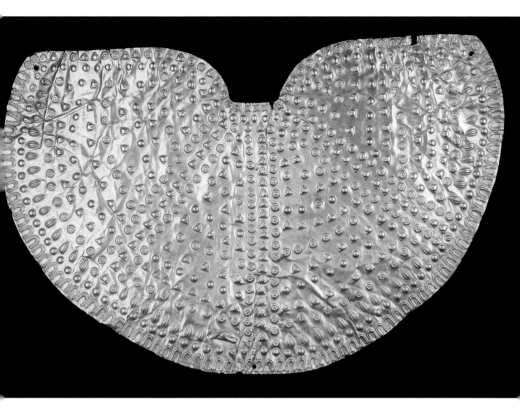

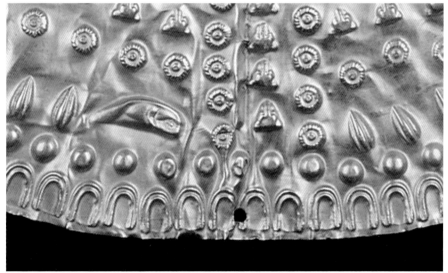

Plate 23

Bronze cuirass

The cuirass was designed to protect a warrior's upper body, and the decoration reflects in stylised fashion the musculature of a male torso on both the breast- and backplate. Both pieces are made of beaten bronze, and they would have been held together with leather straps, which have not survived. Patches made from strips of rivetted bronze on both parts of the cuirass which even show signs of two phases of repair suggest that the cuirass had enjoyed a long existence above ground before burial during the second half of the fifth century. Body armour of the same kind appear on the Siphnian Treasury at Delphi, but is described in a painting by Polygnotus of Thasos in the Lesche of the Cnidians in the same sanctuary: 'such corselets were worn in the olden times,' wrote the traveller Pausanias in the second century AD. 'They consisted of two bronze pieces called *guala*: one fitted the breast and the parts about the belly; the other was meant to protect the back. One was put on in front, the other behind; then they were joined by buckles' (Book 10, 26.2). Rudimentary palmettes incised below the line indicating the thorax have been taken as an indication of local Thracian manufacture: the bronze-smith having given a token lip-service to the more elaborate Greek prototypes he was copying. It is a variant which has been developed to give greater freedom to the head and neck to make it more suitable for use when riding. Horses were a marker of wealth in antiquity, a fact that is in keeping with the generally high status of the goods in the Dalboki tomb.

AN 1948.97. (Breast plate) H.: 35.4cm; W.: 28.8cm. AN 1948.98. (Back plate) H.: 33.6cm; W.: 31.5cm. Lit.: Prochorov 1880, pl. 3.1–2; Filov 1931–32, 53, 55, No. 7; Ashmolean 1948, 20; Dimitrov 1950, 211–12, figs. 4–5, No. 1; Ognenova 1961, 527; *Thracian Treasures* 94, No. 552; Vasilev 1981; Taylor 1985.

Plate 24

Bronze vessel (situla)

This bronze bucket is similar in shape to the silver beakers from Dalboki, a similarity which once led to the suggestion that it was an outsize beaker, 'passed round as a loving-cup at Thracian drinking bouts'. Perhaps; but closer examination reveals the indentations at the rim where the handles of the bucket were once attached, handles which in turn were decorated with palmettes (the 'shadows' of which can still be seen on the surface). A good parallel is the slightly later handled situla from the Mezek tomb, whose extant palmettes are somewhat more elaborate.

AN 1948.99. H.: 27.9cm; D.: 27cm. Lit.: Prochorov 1880, pl. 3.5; Filov 1931–32, 51, 55, No. 5; Ashmolean 1948, 20; Dimitrov 1950, 216, 219, fig. 12, No. 6, 239, n. 15 (list of parallels from elsewhere in Bulgaria); *Thracian Treasures* 94, No. 555. The Mezek situla: Danov and Ivanov 1980, 66, 69, pl. 27.

Bronze bowl

Cast bronze, with lathe-finished grooves at the rim. The wish-bone shaped handles were also cast; one is now missing. The base rests on three bobbin-shaped feet. The handles can be paralleled on bronze bowls from Ezerovo, Ajazlar, and Trebenishte, while the base is of a kind perhaps most familiar from a mosaic at Pompeii of doves perching on a bronze bowl with an egg-and-tongue decoration on the rim, like those on our hydria (plate 25).

AN 1948.100. H.: 10cm; D.: 25.5cm. Lit.: Prochorov 1880, pl. 3.6; Filov 1931–32, 51–3, 55, No. 6; Ashmolean 1948, 20; Dimitrov 1950, 216–17, 220, fig. 13, No. 7 (and for handle parallels: 221–22, figs 16–1); Vocotopoulou 1975, 733.

Plate 25

Bronze water-jar (hydria)
This is the simplest type of a Greek bronze *hydria*; the only adornment is the egg-and-tongue decoration on the rim. The vertical and side handles are of the plainest kind. More elaborate *hydriai* have sirens or other motifs at the base of the vertical handle. Water jars (probably silver) similar in shape to ours can be seen carried on the Parthenon frieze. An identical vessel was found in a Thracian tomb at Duvanli, and five *hydriai* (four plain, one siren) were among 14 Greek bronze vessels found in the vicinity of a wooden boat at Pishchane, Ukraine.

AN 1948.101. H.: 40.5cm; W.: 31.3cm. Lit.: Prochorov 1880, pl. 2.1, 6; Filov 1931–32, 50–1, 55, No. 4; Ashmolean 1948, 20; Dimitrov 1950, 215–16, fig. 8, No. 4; *Thracian Treasures* 94, No. 554. Parthenon frieze: North VI 16–19; Duvanli *hydria*: Filov and Velkov 1930, 313, fig. 34; Pishchane: Ganina 1970.

Plate 26

Silver beaker

The beaker was made from beaten silver, and is decorated with incised ornament: above, lotus blossoms alternating with palmettes, scale ornament, and a guilloche; below, three rows of scale ornament. The underside has an elaborate floral decoration, with a stamped centre. The shape can be paralleled elsewhere in Thrace and Macedonia: earlier examples from Trebenishte, and a later silver beaker from Boukyovtsi; and in Attic pottery heavily influenced by Persian silverware.

AN 1948.102. H.: 11.3cm; D.: 8.4cm; Wt: 183.8 g. Lit.: Prochorov 1880, pl. 2.5, 5.1–2; Filov 1931–32, 47–9, 55, No. 2; Ashmolean 1948, 20, pl. 3 left; Dimitrov 1950, 218, 223, fig. 19, No. 9; Strong 1966, 85, pl. 18, left; *Thracian Treasures* 94, No. 549; Vickers 1992, 62–3, fig. 9; Vickers and Gill 1996, 49–50, n. 137, fig. 2.5, 127, fig. 5.18. Trebenishte beaker: Filov 1927, 6, 31, pl. 6.2; Boukyovtsi beaker: *Thracian Treasures* 61, No. 266; Attic pottery: Gill 1986, 19, 24, fig. 29; Miller 1997, 144, figs. 34, 51.

Silver beaker

Similar to the last, but the lotus and palmette ornament at the top is less accomplished. The scale ornament at the bottom is much the same, but the floral on the underside is much rougher. Said to be a local imitation of 1948.102, but matters may be more complex. The three beakers from Dalboki form a nesting set (with the Hermitage piece fitting between the two beakers in Oxford), and their total weight comes close to the equivalent of 100 Persian silver coins. The shortfall may be accounted for by the wear visible on the underside of the larger Oxford beaker. The three vessels together had long served as a unit of 100 *sigloi*.

AN 1948.103. H.: 12.1cm; D.: 9.4cm; Wt: 183.2 g. Lit.: Prochorov 1880, pls. 2.4, 5.3–4; Filov 1931–32, 47–9, 55, No. 2; Ashmolean 1948, 20, pl. 3 right; Dimitrov 1950, 218, 225, fig. 21, No. 10; Strong 1966, 85, pl. 18, right; *Thracian Treasures* 94, No. 550; Vickers 1992, 62–3, fig. 8; Vickers and Gill 1996, 49–50, n. 137, fig. 2.5, 127, fig. 5.18. Hermitage beaker: Grach 1985, 16–19, No. 9.

Plate 27

Silver mug

The mug is hammered from a single sheet of silver: the centre-point can still be seen on the underside (over-energetic cleaning has created a hole at this point). The bottom is flat, there is a simple moulding at the bottom, the body is bulbous, and the lip turs outwards. The handle was made separately and was hammered on to the rim, but is unattached at its lower extremity. There is a graffito ΣKY incised underneath: an abbreviation perhaps for skyphos (the name of a drinking vessel), or perhaps for the proper name Skythes. The weight of the mug is equivalent to 60 Persian sigloi, allowing for some wear. When the mug arrived in Oxford it, and the silver beakers, were coal black – an effect which was tolerated in antiquity, and which Athenian potters tried to evoke with black gloss.

AN 1948.104. H.: 9cm; D.: 9.5cm; Wt: 327 g. Lit.: Prochorov 1880, pl. 2.10; Filov 1931–32, 50, 55, No. 3; Ashmolean 1948, 20, pl. 3, centre; Dimotrov 1950, 222, fig. 18; Ashmolean 1951, pl. 40; Strong 1966, 85, pl. 18, centre; *Thracian Treasures* 94, No. 551; Oliver 1977, 30, No. 5; Johnston 1978; Vickers and Gill 1996, 122, fig. 5.16.

Plate 28

Two Athenian black-gloss pottery cups

The two black-glossed stemless cups (1947.333 [*above*] is somewhat restored) are a variation of the more common plain-rimmed versions of the 'Delicate class'. The stamped ornament inside consists of a central rosette, a band of palmettes, and a band of tongues. The undersides have series of concentric raised rings – compare the Nymphaeum cup (Plate 15, above), and are glazed black – again evoking a silver model. The cups probably belonged to the same batch and were decorated with the same palmette stamp. They should be dated to ca. 430 BC.

AN 1947.333. Presented by Sir John Beazley. D.: 18.2cm. AN 1948.105. D.: 18.6 cm; Lit.: Prochorov 1880, 5, pls. 3.9, 4.2; Filov 1931–32, 54, 56, No. 12; Ashmolean 1948, 20; Dimitrov 1950, 226, fig. 24; Beazley Gifts (1967), 110, pl.58, No. 414; *Thracian Treasures* 94, Nos. 557–8; Gill 1986, pl. 68, Nos J348–9.

Thracian pottery bowl

Local grey fabric, single horizontal handle, and with a narrow conical foot. Originally, there were two Thracian bowls, the other being somewhat smaller, but it is now lost. It has been said of Thracian pottery that it is 'nothing extraordinary from an artistic point of view'. In Greece there was a close dependence on the part of fine pottery on silverware, but Thracian pottery was rarely given the kind of decoration to be found on the gold and silver vessels of the rich; nor does it often evoke the forms of vessels of precious metal.

AN 1948.107. H.: 8.9cm; D.: 16.8cm. Lit.: Prochorov 1880, 5, pl. 3.7; Filov 1931–32, 53–4, 56, No. 12; Ashmolean 1948, 20; Dimitrov 1950, 222, 227, fig. 25, No. 14; *Thracian Treasures* 94, No. 559. The lost bowl: Prochorov, pl. 3, 8; Filov, 53, 56, No. 11; Dimitrov 1950, 212, 222–3, No. 15.

Plate 29

Iron candelabrum

With tripod feet, and surmounted by a flat disk to support a lamp. The hooks were for hanging a wine-strainer, ladles or further lamps. Iron rarely fares well in the archaeological record, and most surviving lampstands are of bronze. Other relatively complete iron specimens are known from Marion in Cyprus.

AN 1948.109. H.: 76.2cm. Lit.: Prochorov 1880, pl. 2.6; Filov 1931–32, 53, 55, No. 8; Ashmolean 1948, 20; Dimitrov 1950, 223; Rutkowski 1979, 207–8, n. 127 (for bronze candelabra found in Bulgaria and Macedonia), fig. 39. Marion examples: Bailey 1996, 90, No. Q3865.

Iron spearheads

Iron spearheads are, however, regularly found in graves in the Balkans. Notable examples are those from Trebenishte and Vergina.

AN 1948.109. L.: 25cm; Lit.: Prochorov 1880, pl. 3.4; Filov 1931–32, 53, 55, No. 9; Ashmolean 1948, 20; Dimitrov 1950, 212. Trebenishte spearheads: Filov 1927,

Athenian black gloss pottery amphora

This pot is technically 'black gloss' ware, but has been so poorly fired that it looks reddish. It was made at Athens probably in the first half of the fifth century. The presence in the Dalboki tomb of material that is distinctly earlier in date (this amphora, and the cuirass) than the latest (the black-gloss cups of *c.* 430 BC) has been attributed to the occupant having been very old when he died, and buried with objects he had owned for some decades.

AN 1948.108. H.: 36.7cm. Lit.: Prochorov 1880, pl. 2.3; Filov 1931–32, 53, 55, No. 10; Ashmolean 1948, 20; Dimitrov 1950, 218, fig. 11, No. 5; *Thracian Treasures* 94, No. 556. Cf. Sparkes and Talcott 1970, 47, fig. 2, pl. 1, No. 2. Age of deceased: Taylor 1985, 295–7.

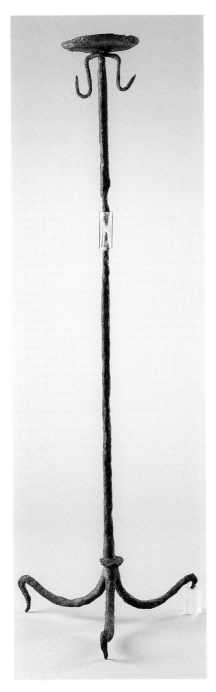

Bibliography

Ashmolean (1948), *Annual Report of the Visitors* 1948 (Oxford).

Ashmolean (1951), *Ashmolean Museum, Department of Antiquities, A Summary Guide* (Oxford).

Beazley, J. D. (1920), *Lewes House Gems* (Oxford).

Beazley, J. D. (1963), *Attic Red-figure Vase painters,* second edition (Oxford).

Beazley Gifts (1967), Ashmolean Museum, *Select Exhibition of Sir John and Lady Beazley's Gifts, 1912–1966* (London).

Becatti, G. (1955), *Oreficerie antiche* (Rome).

Bibikova, B. I. (1970), 'Fauna from the settlements in the village of Kirovo', [В. И. Бибикова, 'Фауна из поселения у с. Кирово'], in Leskov 1970, 97–112.

Bilimovich, Z. A. (1978), 'Etruscan bronze wine strainers found on the Northern Black Sea coast', *On the History of the Northern Black Sea Coast in Antiquity,* ed. K. S. Gorbunova [З. А. Билмович, 'Етрусские бронзовые ситечки найденные в Северном Причерноморье', *Из истории Северного Причерноморья в античную эпоху*, ред. К. С. Горбунова], 26–36 (Leningrad).

Biller, F. (1868), Manuscript account of the excavation of graves at Nymphaeum in December 1868, preserved in the Department of Antiquities, Ashmolean Museum, Oxford.

Boardman, J. (1970), *Greek Gems and Finger Rings* (London).

Boardman, J. and M. L. Vollenweider (1978), *Catalogue of the Engraved Gems and Finger Rings in the Ashmolean Museum* 1, Greek and Etruscan (Oxford).

Cesano, S. L. (1937), 'Bronzetto etrusco inedito a rovescio liscio' *Scritti in onore di Bartolomeo Nogara* (Vatican City) 89–93, pl. 10.

Chernenko, E. V. (1965), 'A leather cuirass of the Scythian period', *Archaeology* [Е. В. Черненко, 'Шкірані панцри скіфсього часу', *Археология*] (Kiev) 17, 144–52.

Chernenko, E. V. (1966), 'On helmets from Nymphaeum', *Soviet Archaeology* [Е. В. Чернеико, 'О шлеме из Нимфея', *Советская археология*] 4, 194–6.

Chernenko, E. V. (1970), 'Burials with weapons in the necropolis at Nymphaeum' [Е. В. Черненко, 'Погребения с оружием из некрополя Нимфея'] in: Leskov 1970, 190–8.

Chernenko, E. V. (1981), *Scythian Archers* [Е. В. Черненко, *Скифские лучники*] (Kiev).

C[h]ernenko, E. V. (1983), *The Scythians, 700–300 BC* (London).

Chester, G. J. (1884), *Notes on the present and future of the archaeological collections of the University of Oxford* (Oxford).

Coche de la Ferté (1956), *Les bijoux antiques* (Paris).

Dimitrov, D. P. (1950), 'Trouvailles funéraires de Dalboki, arr. de Stara-Zagora,' *Fouilles et recherches du Musée National Bulgare,* new series 4, 207–47.

Evans, A. E. (1884), *The Ashmolean*

Museum as a home of archaeology in Oxford (London).

Filov, B. (1927), *Die archaische Nekropole von Trebenischte am Ochrida-See* (Berlin).

Filov, B. (1930–31), 'Das antike Steingrab von Důlboki, Regierungsbez. Stara-Zagora' [Б.Филов, 'Аитична гробица при с. Дълбоки Старозагорско'], *Bulletin de l'Institut archéologique* 6, 45–56.

Fossing, P. (1940), *Glass Vessels before Glass-blowing* (Copenhagen).

From the Lands of the Scythians, Metropolitan Museum of Art Bulletin 32/5 (1973–74), [Exhibition catalogue].

Furtwängler, A. (1900), *Antike Gemmen* (Leipzig/Berlin).

Gajdukevič, V.P. (1971), *Das Bosporanische Reich* (Berlin/Amsterdam).

Galanina, L. and N.Grach (1986), *Scythian Art: the Legacy of the Scythian World, mid-seventh to third century BC* (Leningrad).

Ganina, O.D. (1970), *Ancient Bronzes from Pishchane* [О.Д.Ганина, *Антични бронзи з Пищаного*], (Kiev).

Gardner, E.A. (1884), 'Ornaments and armour from Kertch in the New Museum at Oxford', *Journal of Hellenic Studies* 5, 62–73, pls. 46–47.

Gill, D.W.J. (1986), 'Classical Greek fictile imitations of precious metal vases', in: *Pots and Pans. Proceedings of the Colloquium on Precious Metal and Ceramics in the Islamic, Chinese and Greco-Roman Worlds, Oxford 1985*, ed. M.Vickers (Oxford) 9–30.

Gill, D.W.J. (1986), *Attic Black-glazed Pottery in the Fifth Century B.C.: Workshops and Export*. Oxford: D.Phil. diss.

Gjerstad E. *et al.* (1937), *The Swedish Cyprus Expedition* iii (Stockholm).

Grach, N.L. (1985), *Ancient Decorative Silverware* [Н.Л.Грач, *Античное художественное серебро*] (Leningrad).

Grach, N.L. (1999), *The Necropolis at Nymphaeum* [Н.Л.Грач, *Некрополя Нимфея*] (St Petersburg).

Grose, D.F. (1989), *The Toledo Museum of Art: Early Ancient Glass* (New York).

Hadaczek, K. (1903), *Die Ohrschmuck der Griechen und Etrusker* (Vienna).

Harden, D.B. (1968), 'Ancient glass. i: pre-Roman', *Archaeological Journal* 125, 46–72.

Hermann, W. (1966), 'Archäologische Grabungen und Funde im Bereich der Soprintendenzen von Apulien, Lucanien, Calabrien und Salerno von 1956 bis 1965', *Archäologischer Anzeiger* 81 (Berlin), 255–367.

Himmelmann, N. (1971), *Archäologisches zum Problem der griechischen Sklaverei* (Mainz).

Higgins, R.A. (1961), *Greek and Roman Jewellery* (London).

Hoffmann, H. (1977), 'Sexual and asexual pursuit: a structuralist approach to Greek vase painting', *Royal Anthropological Institute of Great Britain and Ireland, Occasional Paper* 34.

Jacobsthal, P. and A.Langsdorf (1929), *Die Bronzeschnabelkannen: ein Beitrag zur Geschichte des vorrömischen Imports nördlich der Alpen* (Berlin/Wilmersdorf).

Jacobsthal, P. (1931), *Die melischen Reliefs* (Berlin).

Johnston, A.W. (1978), 'Some non-Greek ghosts', *Bulletin of the Institute of Classical Studies* 25, 79–84.

Kulatova, I.N. and A.B. Suprunenko (1996), 'The earliest kurgan at Mgar', in *The Site of Bielsk* (eds. P.K. Bondarevski *et al.*) [И.Н.Кулатова, Супруненко, А.Б., 'Первый мгарский курган', *Більське Городище* (ред. П.К. Бондаревський и др.)] (Poltava) 318–38.

Kunina, N., T.Scholl, O.Sokolova, A.Wąsowicz, (1994 [1995]), 'The bibliography of Nymphaion', *Archeologia* (Warsaw) 45, 79–89; supplements: 46 (1995 [1996]) 89–91, 50 (1999 [2000]) 83–5.

Kunze, E. (1951), 'Etruskische Bronzen in Griechenland', *Studies present-*

ed to D.M.Robinson i (St Louis) 736–46.

Leskov, A.M. (1970), *Antiquities from the Eastern Crimea* [А.М.Лесков, *Древности восточного Крыма*] (Kiev).

Leskov, A.M. (1974), 'Die skythischen Kurgane. Die Erforschung der Hügelgraber Südrusslands', *Antike Welt* 5, Sondernummer.

Lippold, G. (1922), *Gemmen und Kameen* (Stuttgart).

Lyutsenko, A. (1869), Report to the President of the Imperial Archaeological Commission, 3 April 1869. Manuscript [with appended list of drawings by the 'Painter Gross'] in the Archive of the Institute of Archaeology in St Petersburg: Ф. I, 1867 г.; д II, л. 101–2.

Lyutsenko, A. (1870), 'Excavations of tumuli in the locality assumed to be ancient Nymphaeum', *Transactions of the Moscow Archaeological Society* [А.Люценко, 'Раскопки в курганах находящихся на предполагаемой местности древней Нимфеи', *Древности: Труды Московского археологического общества*] 2, 54–5.

Metzler, D. (1971), *Porträt und Gesellschaft* (Munster).

Mertens, J. (1976), 'A Hellenistic find in New York', *Metropolitan Museum Journal* 11, 71–84.

Miller, M. (1997), *Athens and Persia in the fifth century BC: a study in cultural receptivity* (Cambridge).

Minns, E.H. (1913), *Scythians and Greeks* (Cambridge).

Miroshina, T.V. (1977), 'Concerning a type of Scythian coiffure' *Soviet Archaeology* [Т.В.Мирошина, 'Об одном типе скифских головных уборов' *Советская археология*] 3, 79–94.

Morgan, C. (1999), 'A catalogue of Attic pottery in the collection of the Taman Museum', *Taman Antiquity* 2, 1–107 (St Petersburg).

Nawotka, K. (2000 [2001]), 'A graffito of Nymphaion in the Ashmolean Museum', *Archaeologia* (Warsaw) 51, 131.

Nestler, G. and E.Formigli (1993), *Etruskische Granulation. Eine antike Goldschmiedetechnik* (Siena).

Newby, M. (2001), *Glass of four millennia* (Oxford).

Ognenova, L. (1961), 'Les cuirasses de bronze trouvées en Thrace', *Bulletin de correspondance hellénique* 85, 501–38.

Oliver, A., Jr, (1977), *Silver for the Gods*, [Exhibition catalogue] (Toledo, Ohio, etc.).

Onaiko, N.A. (1966), 'Classical Imports into the areas along the Dneiper and Bug Rivers in the seventh–fifth Centuries BC', *Collection of Archaeological Sources* [Н.А.Онайко, 'Античный импорт в Приднепровье и Побужье в VII–V вв до н.э'. *Свод археологических источников*] (Moscow).

Or des Scythes (1975), [Exhibition catalogue] (Paris).

Pharmakowsky, B. (1913), 'Archäologische Funde im Jahre 1912: Russland', *Archäologischer Anzeiger* 178–233.

Platz-Horster, G. (2001), *Altes Museum: Antiker Goldschmuck: Eine Auswahl der ausgestellten Werke* (Berlin).

Pole, W. (1888), *The Life of Sir William Siemens* (London).

Portratz, J.A.H. (1963), *Die Skythen in Südrussland* (Basel).

Prochorov, V. (1880), *Bulgarian excavations in Eski-Zagra* [В.Прохоров, *Болгарские расконки близ Эски-Загры*] (St Petersburg).

Richter, G.M.A. (1961–62), 'The Greek portraits of the fifth century B.C.', *Rendiconti della Pontificia Accademia Romana di Archeologia* 34, 37–57.

Richter, G.M.A. (1968), *Engraved Gems of the Greeks and the Etruscans* (London).

Rolle, R. (1989), *The World of the Scythians* (London).

Rostovtzeff, M. (1922), *Iranians and Greeks in South Russia* (Oxford).

Rostovtzeff, M. (1929), *The Animal Style in South Russia and China* (Princeton).

Rostovtzeff [Rostowzew], M. (1931), *Skythien und der Bosporus* (Berlin).

Rutkowski, B. (1979), 'Griechischer Kandelaber', *Jahrbuch des deutschen Archäologisches Instituts* 94, 174–222.

Ryder, M.L. and Hedges, J.W. (1973), 'Ancient Scythian wool from the Crimea', *Nature* 242, 480.

Scholl, T. and Zin'ko V.N. (1999), *Archaeological map of Nymphaion (Crimea)* (Warsaw).

Shefton, B. (1996), 'Castulo cups in the Aegean, the Black Sea area, and the Near East, with the respective hinterland', in *Sur les traces des Argonautes*, ed. A.Fraysse *et.al.*, 163–86 (Besançon).

Shramko, B.A. (1970), 'On the manufacture of gold ornaments by Scythian craftsmen' *Soviet Archaeology* [Б.А.Шрамко, 'Об изготовлении золотых украшении ремеленниками Скифии', *Советская археология*] 2, 217–221.

Silantyeva, L.F. (1959), 'Necropoleis at Nymphaeum', Materials for Research on the Archaeology of the USSR [Л.ф.Силантьева, 'Некрополь Нимфея', *Материалы и исследования по археологии СССР*] 69, 5–107.

Sparkes, B.A. and Talcott, L. (1970) *Black and Plain Pottery, The Athenian Agora* 12 (Princeton, N.J.).

Strong, E. (1908), 'Antiques in the collection of Sir Francis Cook, Bart., at Doughty House, Richmond', *Journal of Hellenic Studies* 28, 1–45.

Strong, D.E. (1966), *Greek and Roman Gold and Silver Plate* (London).

Talbot Rice, T. (1957), *The Scythians* (London).

Taylor G.L. and Scarisbrick, D. (1978), *Finger Rings from Ancient Egypt to the Present Day* (Oxford).

Taylor, T. (1985), 'Palmettes on the cuirass from Dalboki', *Oxford Journal of Archaeology* 4, 293–304.

Taylor T. (1996), 'Scythian and Sarmatian art', in J.Turner (ed.), *Macmillan Dictionary of Art* 28 (London), 319–326.

Taylor, T. (2001a), 'Thracians, Scythians and Dacians 800 BC–AD 300', in B.W.Cunliffe (ed.), *The Oxford Illustrated History of Prehistoric Europe*, 373–410.

Taylor, T. (2001b), 'Believing the ancients: quantitative and qualitative dimensions of slavery and the slave trade in later prehistoric Eurasia', *World Archaeology* 33, 27–43.

Treasures (1978), M.Vickers, *Scythian Treasures in Oxford* (Oxford).

Vasilev, V.P. (1981),'Ausbesserung von Rüstungen als spezialler Teil der Metallbearbeitung in Thrakien im 5.–3. Jh v. Chr.', *Dritter internationaler thrakologischer Kongress, Wien 1980* (Sofia) 2, 346–65.

Vickers, M. (1981), 'Recent acquisitions of Greek antiquities by the Ashmolean Museum', *Archäologischer Anzeiger*, 541–61.

Vickers, M. (1987), 'Skythische Grabfunde im Ashmolean Museum, Oxford', *Antike Welt* 18/4, 43–50.

Vickers, M. (1992), 'The metrology of gold and silver plate in classical Greece', *The Economics of Cult in the Ancient Greek World*, ed. T.Linders and B.Alroth (Uppsala) 53–72.

Vickers, M. (1999a), *Skeuomorphismus, oder die Kunst aus wenig viel zu machen* (16. *Trierer Winckelmannsprogramm* 1998), (Mainz).

Vickers, M. (1999b) *Images on Textiles: the Weave of Fifth-Century Athenian Art and Society* (*Xenia: Konstanzer Althistorische Vorträge und Forschungen,* Heft 42) 1999).

Vickers, M. and D.Gill (1996), *Artful Crafts: Ancient Greek Silverware and Pottery*, second edn (Oxford).

Vickers, M., O.Impey and J.Allan (1986), *From Silver to Ceramic: the Potter's Debt to Metalwork in the*

Greco-Roman, Chinese and Islamic Worlds (Oxford).

Vickers, M. and A. Kakhidze (2001), 'The British-Georgian Excavation at Pichvnari, 1998: the "Greek" and "Colchian" cemeteries', *Anatolian Studies* 51, 65–90.

Vocotopoulou, J. (1975), 'Le trésor de vases de bronze de Votonisi', *Bulletin de correspondance hellénique* 99, 729–88.

Wild, J.P. (1978), 'Classical Greek textiles from Nymphaeum', *Journal of the Textile Museum* 4, 4, 334.

Williams, D., and Ogden, J. (1994), *Greek Gold: Jewellery of the Classical World* (London).

Zgusta L. (1955), *Die Personennamen griechische Städte der nördlichen Schwarzmeerküste* (Prague).